My Darling, Delirium.

Kabrie Waters

Printed in the United States of America

First Printing, 2019

ISBN 978-1-949321-04-3
Library of Congress Control Number: 2019937803

All writings and images within this compilation are the
property of Kabrie Waters, or other artists as indicated.
A.B.Baird Publishing has the explicate right to use all
writings and work of art included within this work for
this work alone. Contributing authors and artists
maintain the copyrights for each piece submitted and
published within book.

Cover Art By: Michael Lilley

Photography by Kabrie Waters and Rainie Foerester
unless otherwise indicated

A.B.Baird Publishing
66548 Highway 203
La Grande OR, 97850
USA

www.abbairdpublishing.com

Table of Contents

Table of Contents Continued

Table of Contents Continued

MY DARLING, DELIRIUM

The vinyl has been skipping for hours now...
playing itself over and over
in a form of melancholic masturbation,
it's every scar fondled repeatedly
by the needle.
The light has been flickering for days
and the walls perform a balancing act,
leaning from black to white
on an unstable wire.
And I let them be.
Everything requires an identity crisis to be something
I suppose.
And I speculate...
with my coal colored glasses
and insistent uncertainty.
How long have I been laying here?
You've been gone for months now
but still you mock me with your absence.
Until I start to see you in reflective surfaces,
an optical illusion with homicidal tendencies.
I can no longer differentiate
between the lingering scent of whiskey
and my own perfume...
and I wonder if I'll always smell of sadness now.
Though the thought is romantic,
and almost appealing,
I remember that I'm too stubborn
to let the world see me bent...
and too prideful to admit that maybe..
you've broken me.
I can't remember the last time I ate
but in a sick way I like the feeling
of cold water flooding my empty stomach
Like copper coins bouncing
off the sides of a wishing well.

Will I only ever be made up of wishes now?
Will all of them wear your face
like a maddening masquerade?
There's a knock at the door
or perhaps a hopeful figment
of a hungry imagination.
You see, I've been listening to the constant buzz of the
ceiling fan so intently
that now,
like a siren it sings to me
and the voices of those I care for
are neither menacing nor melodic enough
to pull me from my trance.
I thought I was crazy before
but now, having misplaced my mind
somewhere in a mold infested basement...
The thought no longer scares me.
It might be nice to fade into the furniture
and wilt with the pedals
and break with the dishes
and soften with the screams...
I've been having bad dreams...
but not like I used to, no...
In these I am painfully awake
and mostly alive
but nothing has changed
and I wake only to find my reality
mimicking my worst fears.
You finally walk away.
And how could I blame you?
How can I dissolve and expect you to stay?
I've become an almost living,
barely breathing anesthetic...
and I think I understand now...

Numbness is far more fatal than pain.

EVANESCENT

You're turning into a memory,
Your lines are blurring
and features fading.
It's like waking up from a dream...
and frantically trying to fall back asleep,
fast enough to find it...
only to lie awake missing something just beyond
memory.
I'm forgetting the mornings
I tried so hard to hold onto...
I studied the sunlight draped along your face...
but trying to see it now,
is like catching clouds
from the wrong side of a plane window on it's way to
Santa Fe.
The more I try to feel what I once did when I was yours...
the more it eludes me.
I know we weren't good for each other...
but there are parts of me
that just aren't ready to let you go.

Diamond
I became what you molded me to be. I became beautiful,
Elegant, statuesque with every brush stroke.
I was lovely, and cold like dead flowers you hung from a wall
You made diamonds from coal...
and wondered why they wouldn't keep you warm.

SELF EXPECTATION

If I turn the music up loud enough
maybe it will deafen me to the disappointment.
If I drink the wine quick enough
maybe I can make my demons dizzy.
If I scrub every fucking surface in this house
till my fingerprints fall down the drain,
just maybe...
The glare beaming from behind layers of dust
will blind me long enough to make me forget
where I am.
Who I am.
And how different it was all supposed to be.

A STRANGE ALCHEMY

"I Love you more" he said,
and he's probably right.
Love is a chemical in the brain that my body
refuses to produce with the same negligence it once did.
But even with my faulty wiring,
I will continue to love you in whatever artificial way I
am able.
With my best efforts
and a strange alchemy,
I am yours.

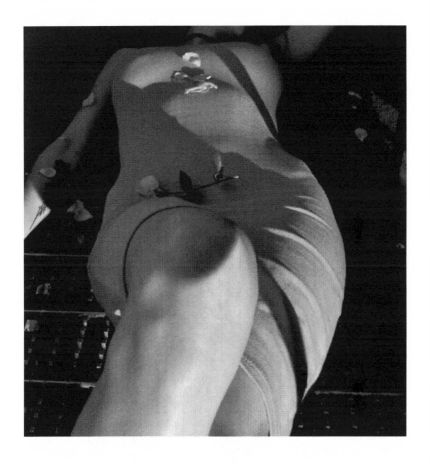

The Creation Of
Why, when I call you beautiful,
does it sound more like an apology than a compliment?
My Dear, I know all too well of the chaos
that goes into the creation of creatures like you.
The horrors that made you...
they made me too.

WHERE I NEEDED ACCEPTANCE,
YOU OFFERED REPAIRS

Am I to blame for the baggage that fills this house from
floor to ceiling?
Did I invite the nightmares that share our bed?
Would I still feel whole,
had I not been taught to be polite?
Where I needed acceptance, you offered repairs,
but could I have kept myself from being broken to begin
with?
Would you be offended if I said I didn't know how to
love anymore?
That any depth I had was filled in for my own self
preservation?
Would you find me mad,
If loneliness bothers me less that crowds of people
with the same face, and no names?
Where I needed acceptance, you offered repairs...
and I couldn't help but laugh as you tried to glue the
pages back together...
because though I may read like a warning label now...
I've gotten used to the way
my pages are rearranged.

FROM DAY TO DAY

Tomorrow,
It's the girl reading Faulkner in the coffee shop corner...
with her pastel shirt,
and glasses that don't quite fit her face.

Next week,
It's the boy downtown,
sitting cross legged in the way of foot traffic,
sketching a flower bed
before returning to his bank job.

Yesterday my dear,
It was you...
with your photographs
and coffee stains on tailored suits.
Yesterday, it was you,
From New York, to Montana,
to that basement apartment we rarely left.
Yesterday it was you...

Today...
It has to be me.
With my contradictions and fickle mind.

It is me,
walking alone in cemeteries,
imagining the lives marked on headstones.
It is me, with my stacks of unfinished poems
and the clean laundry I leave in the same spot on the
floor...

I know I'll have love to give again.
I fall in love with strangers every day...
but right now, in this moment...
it is me...
and the love I am learning
to give myself.

Marks

Days like this I'm just another poem in a world that's lost its taste for poetry.
Days like this I'm the leaf that fell into freshly poured cement.
Days like this Though I know I've made my mark on the world,
I wonder if it was worth the marks
the world has made on me.

PHOENIX

She drenched herself in gasoline,
and wore it like a ball gown.
She felt it wrap around her every curve
and I know it's morbid,
but it was wondrous.
To see the woman who had so often been burned,
finally ignite.
To Watch her dance in protest through the flames...
like a fucking monk.
I suppose out of spite, or bitterness, or pride...
She decided that if the world was going to kill her,
she would do it herself,
in a far more poetic way.

WHEN I'VE GOTTEN BETTER

I haven't been sleeping much...
which is to say,
I close my eyes and my head starts writing ransom notes.
I've gone a bit mad...
which is to say,
I think my dreams are trying to kill me.
I want to be alone...
which is to say,
I don't want you to see me this way.
Goodbye...
or rather,
please come back to me...
when I've gotten better.

With You

Bury me in sun stained lace curtains.
Leave dried lilacs at my grave.
Let the eulogy read like a concerto.
Let me fade on this golden misty morning.
For all the beauty I need see...
came,
and went
with you.

COME AROUND

Everything you give comes in pieces,
love spent in carefully counted fragments.
Like partial silhouettes
plastered between shadows.
It's an image that could be a promise
or merely, a passing phenomenon.
And of course I mind it...
of course it is disappointing to know
that you will never get quite what you give...
but you,
with your walls and your hesitance
are worth my love.
You...
I have to believe...
will come around.

WITH OR WITHOUT

I don't know how to be without you...
you made sure of that for your own consolation.
I don't want to be with you...
I guess you could say I've outgrown self deprecation.
But you modeled me for so long...
made me your imitation.
And now,
when I'm alone in a room...
you're still there with me,
always just smiling.

People Like Us
Maybe it's people like us, who never imagined
they might be made of anything more than bones and dust.
Those who know how hopeless the world can appear.
Maybe it's people like us,
that were always destined to hang the stars.

IF BLOSSOMS NEVER GROW

I am not what others have done to me.
I am not the fragments of stolen pride
or the dearly departed pieces of self
that I recite eulogies for,
in every. Poem. I. Write.
I am not my past...
and I believe this may be the most painful part.
How haunting is the thought,
that what I am now, may be all that's left.
How do I convince myself that these remains,
are nothing to be ashamed of?
That the pieces I still own,
were too strong, or simply too sharp,
to be taken?
What I mean to say is,
when a vineyard has been ravaged by the flock,
is it not still beautiful somewhere,
somehow in it's decay?
These bare branch limbs may have nothing left to show
but scars,
but do they not still stand?
And if blossoms never grow here again...
perhaps we can both learn to love the debris.
Perhaps I am not quite as broken as I seem.

WHEN YOU LEFT US

Your shirt hung out over the chair.
Ironed, and ready for a day that wouldn't start.
Your newspapers from yesterday morning were still
scattered,
halfway read, around the kitchen table.
An unfinished crossword puzzle was laid to rest in the
glovebox of your car
as it sat like a tombstone in your driveway.
They told me you had left us...
I didn't believe them. I figured it had to be a cruel trick...
because it was all here. Your world was on pause
like a film waiting for the return of its audience.
There were no missing fragments.
No abrupt stop to the sunlight casting shadows through
the windows.
No moment of silence from the blackbirds.
Just rooms...
unchanged,
abandoned,
and somehow colder without you in them.

A Lesson in Self Restraint
He called again today
and I kept conversation on a short leash.
I kept a head count of every syllable
as they marched down my tongue
like prisoners into cells.
When it was time to hang up
I didn't say I loved him...
but I'm not yet as calloused as I'd like him to think I am...
because I still wanted to.

RECOLLECTION

It's hard to remember sometimes
that what I felt for you was real.
But, it must have been once.
It must have been monumental,
for I still commemorate you in most things I do.
I must have believed in us enough
to fight for it,
like soldier to country.
My left over lacerations must surely prove this.
It must have been beautiful,
but I can't quite recall who we were then,
before we became what we are now...
I loved you once...
but I just can't retrieve it,
from where it was buried.

SHOOTING STARS, SILHOUETTES, AND YOU

Obsessions prey upon my mind
and though the loneliness temporarily subsides,
even the most captivating concepts become intrusive.
Like shooting stars, silhouettes, and you.
But if I fixate on trivial commodities...
like decaying reiterations of poetry
or amber leaves clothed in crimson on their deathbeds...
Though my time is often squandered,
it is never spent in solitude.

Maybe I'm The Artist
I'll never be the kind of girl they write songs about.
I'll never be the woman in the painting,
making the world wonder with a simple smile.
I wasn't meant to stand among the muses.
But maybe I'm the artist...
and maybe it's you darling,
I am meant to immortalize.

BORN TO DIE

A requiem was for sung for us,
and our eulogy was recited.
Our names we're etched on slabs of stone...
long before we knew them.
What I felt for you...
What I FEEL for you...
it was born still
with blue cheeks
and recessed lungs.
Fate had its hands at our throats
before I had the chance to kiss your neck
before I held your hand...
before I had a chance to love you...
and the people will say what they will
they will speculate and craft conclusions...
but they can not say we didn't put up a fight.
god damn it, we tried...
and never in human history
have any two people put up such a fight...
I'm sorry though,
that it wasn't enough.

IT'S A MESS

We don't talk about your AA meetings.
Nor do we talk about the atrocities that live in my head.
Because you are addicted to the numbness
and I am addicted to the pain
and somewhere in the middle,
we collide like lost comets.
I help you feel a little more,
you help me feel a little less
and we're a mess...
but somewhere in the clutter is all the pieces
of every nightmare that brought us here.
Every stab wound that shaped our lives.
We're a mess...
but somewhere from the rubble
a castle can be built,
and perhaps from those towers,
we can find a way to heal.

I Wrote Today
I wrote today, for the first time in a long time.
Whether it's a poem or a suicide note...I'm not certain.
But even if it's poorly written.
Even if it sounds like "Goodbye".
Even if it is only ever heard by my walls...
It gives me something to edit tomorrow.
It gives me something to wake up for.

YELLOW SUNDRESS

I wore a yellow sundress,
hoping to catch the attention of someone kind...
but you found me instead.
You, with your house on the hill,
your soundproof windows,
and your paintings that only depict pain.
You who built your four post bed
knowing full well that it's steel limbs
would be strong enough to break my spirits.

I wore a yellow sundress.
You peeled it away from me,
and then my skin,
and then my sanity.
You with a touch that was only gentle
because it knew there would be no fight.
You who handcrafted my nightmares.
You, who I see in every stranger on the street.
You, whose fingerprints have stained my skin.
You, who turned my body into a crime scene
and made me believe that never again could it be my
temple.

You...
whose name I kept from my mother.
You, the father of three...
How can you check for monsters beneath their beds
While you linger below mine with fangs bared and
claws sharpened?

I wore a yellow sundress...
and for the first time in years,
it's threads didn't feel like your hands.
For the first time since then,
I worked up the courage to tell my mother.
For the first time I don't speak of it as though I'm
apologizing.
For the first time...

I wore my yellow sundress,
hoping to catch the attention of someone kind.
And this time...
I know the difference.

INSOMNIA

I sip coffee stronger than I am with the man on the
moon.
we whisper secrets and laugh at the stars listening in,
like the old woman from the corner shop.
I pour my irregular heart beats out to the milky way.
She spins them all in circles until they remember their
rhythm.
I sometimes start to believe that my words have run
dry...
and then the constellations remind me of all the creation
I am capable of.

I'm jealous of the way the steam from my coffee
and the smoke from your cigarette
dance together...
We used to collide that way.

APPR'S MOI LE DE' LUGE
(AFTER ME, THE DELUGE)

You will be left with empty walls
and vacant chairs.
The silence will ensnare you.
For the first time,
you will know the hysteria
that comes from having nothing left to lose.
When I've gone,
the hell that resides in your head
will break loose.
Though there was a time I'd have wept on your behalf...
though there was a time I'd have tried to save you,
you took the last of my sympathy...
along with all else
you felt was owed to you.

EPHEMERAL

The best loves,
or perhaps the most memorable,
are ephemeral.
They aren't meant to last,
but like shooting stars,
you'll not soon forget the way they blazed across your
sky.
Rearranged your universe.
Sent sparks soaring into every dark corner of the cosmos.
And then they simply leave you there...
whirling in an elysium world,
an oblivion,
you'd never dared to imagine.

Bruise
Dwelling on you
is much like applying pressure to a bruise.
It hurts
in that numb-beneath-the-surface
kind of way.
but that pain is the only way I can feel you...
the only fragment I have left...
so I push, and push, and push...
until the pain becomes just another sensation of the flesh.

MUSCLE MEMORY

Defeating your demons is the first step.
Second, understand that it's not us they will hurt now,
but those who choose to love us.
Because like a corpse soaks into the soil
They become a part of who we are.
Unseen, but like a phantom limb,
always a part of our muscle memory.
Always the root of our instincts.
Reminding us of our need to survive,
even in the safest of places.

IF YOU KNEW ME

If you knew me,
you'd know that rings are just crutches I'll let you lean
on.
Like religion.
Like astrology.
Like a promise.
If you knew me,
you'd know that promises are just places
I keep on a bucket list
in the back of a junk drawer.
With rings.
With love letters.
With permanence.
If you knew me,
you'd know that "temporary" is a scenic train ride
to "set in stone".
If you knew me,
you'd know that I can be a coward...
so I lied...
though I told you otherwise...
this
is
goodbye.

Thursday Night Reflections
Looking back, I'd only change that I was the sort of person
who required broken hearts,
for the reparation of their own.
My worst regret will always be
every apology I was strong enough to write...
but never brave enough to send.

I ALMOST DON'T LOVE YOU

I wake up sometime around mid-day
with a whiskey bottle tipped over the edge of the bed,
sending it's last drops like little drunken love letters to
the floor boards.
My throat feels sore but not in a burning way like it does
with vodka...
this feels more like the fleshy walls and vocal chords
have all stuck together
and now I pull them part like strings of licorice
like bananas from their peels...or like I pulled myself
from you.
I was never the epitome of grace, and even now,
 with vomit in my hair and cheap cologne from last
nights bar flies staining my skin,
I know it's not very ladylike of me. I imagine you would
have been disappointed...
a thought that would have once rattled me but now,
wraps me in a strange sense of satisfaction.
I'll admit, I am not handling this very well.
 I never have done well, being alone with myself.
but I didn't call you last night... I almost didn't think of
you.
I almost didn't miss you. and I never thought it possible...
but this boozy blur I've been keeping myself in just
might be working...
and of course it's all because of you… it might even be
for you...
as everything I've done has been… but my dear,
it won't be that way for too much longer… I take
another swallow
and revel in the sting… and I've almost stopped
dreaming of you
I've almost stopped looking for you… I almost don't love
you.

FOREIGN COMFORT

I am not easily friable,
but you have a way of reducing me
back to a viridity,
a vulnerability
I thought I'd locked away within my ribcage.
With the featfull tones pirouetting from your tongue
and the equanimity in the way you calm me...
loving you is ineluctable...
and in that alone,
I have finally found a foreign comfort
in contentment.

Skin

The skin that fits me like a wool sweater
shrunk in the wash.
The skin that I crawl from.
The skin that's been stained,
like a tablecloth with red wine,
by uninvited dinner guests.
The skin I had come to hate.
You kissed my skin… and it felt like mine again.

WORST PARTS

The worst part is,
I really tried this time.
I opened every rusted door
and dusted every skeleton on the shelf.
I introduced you to my demons one by one...
and you said you loved all of me.
You swore I wasn't the monster
statistics said I should be.

The worst part is,
I really tried this time.
Every time I caved and called it compromise...
I fed your dreams the most tender pieces of my own.

The worst part is,
I really tried this time. I loved you so entirely
that when you drained the last of me
I still felt lucky...
to be lying shriveled
in your arms.

STAY

Hold me,
until shadows on my walls look less like wolves.
Kiss me,
until the sharp edges of your lips and mine
finally soften.
Love me,
until airplanes no longer resemble open doors
and suitcases no longer glow like exit signs.
Stay,
until I realize it's always been you
I was running to.

Walls
I let you dismember my walls,
and in return,
you've reminded me why I built them.

CROWS, KITCHEN KNIVES, AND TEENAGE SUICIDE

Crows flocked together in the street,
either flirting with death
or simply enjoying the symbolism.
We sat in silence for a long time,
observing them from the curb...
You said you loved the way they mocked us in that
moment...
Because we gave them made up meaning.
We sat them upon deaths shoulder like a parrot.
and as a jester taunts the king,
 they obliged and finished with a bow.
You said you wondered if they ever wanted to be doves...
just to see what it felt like.
Just to be wanted as something more than a sideshow
oddity.
I wondered what you wanted to be...
I wondered what you were
when you weren't playing a part for the hungry crowds.
When you peek through your mask,
do they offer to hide the kitchen knives?
When you read the statistics, do they spell out your
name?
When you asked to be a dove...
did they tell you
"be happy...
to be a crow".

A POEM WHILE UNPACKING

The life we built together
remains only in remnants.
The antique bell
that still sounds like that first hesitant "I love you".
The imported hand woven rugs we lied upon.
The half used perfume bottles and the memories soaked
in their scents.
The flowers you gave me,
now dried and shedding on a shelf.
This is what's left of us now.
Boxes of objects,
and photos arranged across the floor
like a funeral program
for a love that never got a proper burial.

A Common Misconception
It is a common misconception but
we do not suffer for our art,
suffering is a result of the human condition.
Creation,
is not a side effect of our disease...
it is the cure.
It is often the only thing
that makes looking at ourselves bearable.

COMMITMENT ISSUES

Growing up, we moved a lot.
Names, faces, friends, and houses...
they all passed like polaroids on a conveyor belt.
Stability began to sound too much like loss
and change dangled like an oxygen mask in a plane
crash.
Detachment became a voice in my head, always
whispering with worry when I got too close.
My mothers defences ignite when the subject is
mentioned,
 burning through the conversation till it's nothing but
dust
left to rest upon the shelf another day.
I suppose she blames herself for my inability to make
commitments
but her guilt is misplaced.
I never wished it to be anything more than what it was.
Several years, heartaches, and seemingly reckless
decisions later,
I found myself sprawled across a tile floor, clutching a
melting pot of pills.
All of them with different names,
colors,
and promises of something better.
None of them were created to treat confusion,
or doubt,
or depression,
or my failure to find a fucking purpose to it all.
Had I known how to commit...
Had permanence not started with the same letter as
pain...
I'd have let each pill slide down my throat,
to fill every self inflicted flesh wound.

I'll likely never stay with one person or grow
comfortable in the same place
or make a plan I'll carry out without snapping beneath
its weight.
My commitment issues will keep me lost and lonely...
but they keep me breathing.
They keep my heart half beating
They keep my lips moving for all the lies I have yet to
tell,
and the goodbyes that have yet to torment me.

BROKEN INVENTION

I know your fears grew from the same lonely place as
mine.
The tattoo on your arm is the only permanence you've
known.
But while we're both waiting for the bomb to drop,
dance with me through the air raid.
Remember how the sirens made us sway
and when it all comes crashing down around us,
know that years from now...
a smile will tip-toe across my lips
when my ears start humming the phantom notes
to the song of our own broken invention.

There's a box in the attic
I pull it out now and then,
to look over the hearts I've broken,
the bad decisions,
and other scraps of decorative decay.
I hang it on the walls,
learn to love every ragged piece
and put it away again
until I need to be reminded
that even the hard times have their place
and their purpose.

A REMINDER TO YOU: I AM YOURS

I know you hate finding him in my writing.
I know it hurts you,
that he hides in some of my less desirable habits.
But he was a part of me once,
almost the way you are a part of me now,
but with more delusion.
I see you cringe when our friends speak his name,
but have you noticed that I no longer do?
I imagine you'd like to burn the photos I kept,
but should the past not be preserved?
Left to be a lesson in a dusty display case?
Do we not collect some souvenirs,
to reminds us of the places we elude?
I know it confounds you,
that he ever had me...
but love, just remember,
he had me then...
so you could keep me now.

MY WORLD

My world is made up of canary colored walls,
rust stains, and hazelnut coffee.
It entangles you with fishnet thighs
and lullabies of the broken people.
My world is a crooked music box ballerina,
a flooded basement floor,
and a jade plant in the windowsill that refuse to grow.
My world is not made up of shining city lights,
chandeliers, or chariots ready to whisk you away.
My world is not a fairy tale, or even a poet's melancholic
wonderland...
it is ordinary, and messy, and brutal at times.
But I believe with you in it,
our world could be an enchantment among the
numbered streets.
I believe with you in it, this world could feel like home.

Sometimes you must fall apart.
Just to see what you're made of.

A SMALL LIST OF REASONS WHY

You asked me why I loved you...
and I thought in that moment
of all the things I would miss
if you ever went away.
Like the way your hat rests behind one ear.
The grace in the way you avoid social settings.
The faint smile that sometimes visits in your sleep...
or the way you tell me about your bad dreams.
I'd miss the distant stare that tells me
when your mind is far away,
creating wonders from the dirt at your feet.
I'd miss the songs you send me...
but more so, the ones you sing.
Your ability to turn frozen pizzas and ramen noodles
into works of culinary genius.
I'd miss teasing you about peanut butter-cheese
sandwiches.
You asked me why I loved you...
because never in my life...
did I imagine I'd find someone that fits me...
the way you do.

POSTCARD

Write me a postcard,
from that place you go to when we are lying in bed
and you are staring at the ceiling as if it were made of
glass
and the stars were waltzing across the sky for only you.
Write me a postcard,
From wherever you may be when we are speaking
but you are listening to melodies being sung by sirens
that speak in a language only you know.
Write me a postcard,
From that shore you sail to when my hand is holding
yours
but your fingers are slipping themselves through piles of
fine white sand.
Write me a postcard,
Tell me you don't want me with you wherever you are.
Write me a postcard,
From the place that is far more beautiful than what I was
able to give you.

The people that have hurt you
Are not monsters.
They are human…
And somehow,
That's worse.

NO ON WANTS A RAPE POEM, BUT THEY DON'T STOP THEM FROM BEING WRITTEN EITHER

I thought I had moved on...
I believed I'd spent enough time
crawling from my skin like cockroaches from
floorboards.
I thought I was safe now...
that the nights spent submerged in showers
until the water went cold
had soaked away the crime scene my body had become.
I thought I'd forgotten the details of your face
but your features follow me from the similarities of
strangers.
I've filled my home with candles and drenched my
clothing in perfume
but the smell of your sweat falling to my unwilling body
still robs me on the streets.
I thought I was strong now...
but does it take only strength to tell the ones I love
 that they couldn't protect me?
That I couldn't protect my self?
How do I reclaim something that wasn't given by choice?
How do I tell my story without it reading too much like a
warning label?
I thought I had moved on...
I believed, if I burnt the clothing of a victim
that I could wear the polished suit of a survivor...
How can I call myself a survivor when I still question
what I could have done?
When I still wonder what I did wrong?
How do I leave behind the habits formed in self-defense?
How do I keep still when his hands try to hold me
and all I feel, are your fingerprints embedded in my
flesh?
I thought I had left the wreckage behind me...
but how do you burn a bridge that you never had the
courage to build?

THE GARDENER

Growing up, we didn't have much...
What we did have was our mother,
who was often tired and frail
and looked as though she might cave in at any moment...
but she never did.
She had more fight in her little finger
than most people have in their entire bodies.
She had a way of turning every broken home into a
palace.
So we bought a small house on fourth street.
The yard was barren.
the paint was chipped.
the floors and corners were soaked with mold.
The world looked bleak,
but she scrubbed till her fingers bled.
She painted till her arms trembled.
She planted flowers in every ugly corner...
and she taught us that even in hell,
a home can grow.

Walk cautiously…
There are holes in my alibis.
Pay attention…
Or they will swallow you whole.

TASTE

I wonder what our memories must taste like to you?
Does your tongue start to rust when you think of the
nights spent fighting?
Is it covered in exotic spices when you think of the sex?
Do you remember the coconut tinted kisses?
or the sherbet sunsets we used to watch?
Do you remember the good times?
Or is your enamel stained with everything we wished we
could take back?
Can you see it when we smile?
all the pain stuck between our teeth?
Or will you step back...and swallow all the sweet things
we gave each other?

MISTAKEN

I have confused the sound of your car engine with my
own heart beat.
When you pull up my rib cage starts to rattle from the
violent pounding and every time you pull away there is
an unsettling stillness in my chest.
TThis leaves me wondering if maybe my pulse has
become reliant on you to pump my blood.   I try
not to think of what would happen to my breathing
should the crackling of your tires on the gravel ever
stop.

I have confused the sound of your voice for my favorite
song.
When you speak my body begins to dance without me as
if on a cue I don't remember being given, as though
maybe I was a sleeper agent in a past life and my soul
was trained to move only for yours. But I wonder if I
could remember the steps if you were to stop playing.

I have confused you for a home.
Your arms are a door I feel I can walk into without
having to knock and though I don't take that for granted
I should know by now that people are not building
materials...
They do not make stable shelters.

SYMPHANIES FALL SILENT

Symphonies fall silent
sparks distinguish into ash
and yes, I know even love will always be a fading thing
a fog evaporating into the autumn afternoons...
for people like me, who only appreciate the things they
have yet to find...
but if you don't mind,
may I keep you with me
through photographs and memories
to remind me to listen for as long as the band will play
to be mesmerized while the sparks are dancing,
like fireflies on warm Virginia nights.
To love as entirely
as effortlessly, as you loved me,
regardless of goodbye that follows....
and the suffocating silences that will take your place by
my side.

A Sad Ending to a Story I Cant Write
*My pride urges me to say that we lived happily ever after.
That love overcame all obstacles, and that the odds, stacked
against us like New York City skyscrapers, were irrelevant in
the end. But I am not here to write you a fairytale. I am not
here to give you hope.*

LESSONS IN LOVE

You were worn and weathered when I found you.
I rebuilt your brittle bones with borrowed marrow.
I lent you air leaked from my own lungs.
You said you hadn't felt so young in years but caught up in your rejuvenation,
you failed to realize that the drops of youth I carried to your fountain
were drained from my own.
The years I peeled from your heart had to be held somewhere for safe storage
 and my rib cage had a vacancy.
I am learning that this is what it means to love...
giving someone wings, even if you must clip the feathers from your own.
Teaching someone to fly, even if it means they might leave you.

I was always better at putting myself in someone else's shoes,
Than I was standing in my own.

SOMEDAY

Someday the fireflies
will learn to live in glass jars.

Someday the flowers
will sprout from rusted kitchen sinks.

Someday shoes
will walk down cobblestone streets,
with no one to guide them.

On that day...

I will unpack my suitcase
and stay still, happily,
in one place.

PAINTED GREEN GRASS

You showed me the other side of the tracks
the dead grass was painted vibrant green.
the rotting fence posts painted white.
The broken people smiled
and I wondered,
why I had dreamed of this place all my life.
You showed me the finer things in life,
but the chardonnay was bitter
and the satin sheets felt as cold as you.
You took me to the city I dreamt of from a trailer park...
but nothing was real. and nothing was good...
it all, like you, was just meant to look that way.

My heart gasps at the mere memory of you...
If anyone were to utter your name, I think it might stop beating
all together.
For you were a far better poem,
Than I ever could have written.

WINTER

And as the snow met the ground with a gentle
introduction,
My world turned to stone.
I've been here too long...
I know the street names by heart. I've memorized the
faces.
With nothing new to ignite my mind,
It freezes over.
Now all I can do
Is huddle beneath your promises,
That someday soon
This ice will thaw.

ALONE WITH YOU

Do you know what it's like to live in your shadow?
To feed your fire with coals from my own?
It's Antarctica when the sun burns out.
It's standing naked and bare
In mid-winter sleet
Wondering if there was ever a time
I didn't feel so alone
Being with you.

I know how hard it can be to love someone like me.
I had to learn to love myself,
Long before I let you try.

An old friend once told me,
Writers have a life expectancy of 35.
Strangely this has been the easiest to evasion.
An ending stained with more poetry,
Than life could ever conjure.

I never wanted to hurt you.
But my heart is a landmine, hidden sweetly among the flowers.
And you… were just in the wrong place.
At the wrong time.

DADDY ISSUES

The issue does not root from absence or insecurity.
My father was never absent.
He is in my inherited eyes. He is in my temper.
He is watching proudly at every reckless decision I
make.
He sits in the corners smirking, calling me "sis',
When you call me incapable of love.
He is always in my ear…
Reminding me that no one is to be trusted…
Especially not myself.

We are creatures of want.
Humans controlled by hunger.
Slaves to our need to consume.
We're held captive to hearts
That require the blood of others to beat.
So we hurt the ones we love,
It's human nature in all of its brilliant naivety
To cage what we believe is ours to keep.

I like to believe that even from across the country,
You still smile when you see my footprints on the passenger side
of your windshield.
I like to convince myself…
That you haven't yet washed them away.

TRICKS OF TIME

If tomorrow were a promise,
would we love at all?
Without the fear of dying alone,
Would we ever put our hearts on the line?
If it we're an eternity ahead of us instead of just a
lifetime…
Would I choose to spend it with you?
Would you choose to spend it with me?
With forever to collect all the treasures of life…
Would we still see one another
as something precious enough to keep?

Enlightenment is the heaviest burden to bear...
But the most beautiful thing that will ever break you.

HE ISN'T YOURS

He isn't yours.
He can't be.
As lovely as he is,
As much as he has chiseled away at your icy heart,
You break every beautiful thing you try to hold.
Quit writing false hope along the walls
Of a tomb you've disguised as a tunnel.
Don't tell him that the fumes seeping through his lungs
will help him breathe.
Don't send him to live in the same place you've let
yourself die.
He isn't yours.
He can't be.
You haven't yet learned to love anything
More than yourself.

They will notice the dirt beneath your nails
Before they notice the grave you've just clawed your way out of.

PTSD

You walk like someone that's been through hell.
Your stride shows unworldly strength...
But you keep looking over your shoulder, and I can't help but
wonder...
What could have followed you home?

Contribution Section

(But first, a foreword, as unorthodox as it may be at this juncture of the book.)

*I am honored to introduce to you the works of some very talented artists
that I have come to find throughout this journey.
I can not stress enough the importance
of supporting your fellow creators.
As artists, we bleed, so that the world may heal.
To my supporters, I can not thank you enough for the love
and support you have shown me over the last few years,
this book is dedicated to you.
To all the artists out there, never stop. Never give up on
yourself. Never stop bleeding.
Enjoy!
-K. Waters
Xoxo*

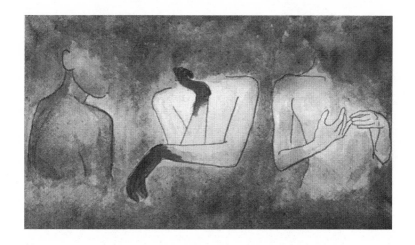

Tomas Larrauri "Violencia"

Tomas Larrauri "Nympheas2"

Lovers at Peace.

In the darkness of your room, your silk blanket shimmers in the moonlight. Earth's nocturnal darlings are composing a symphony that only we know. I hear your heart racing. You feel my body tremble.

You wrap your arms around me and envelope me in your musk, and hold me captive with your gaze.

Your lips taste like heaven. Your body feels like home. As you kiss my neck, we melt into a masterpiece.

We are our own works of art.

When I look in your mirror, *The Kiss* is staring back; vulnerable, emotional, and at peace in the arms of my beloved.

T.J. Jensen – 1/16/2018

Her Eyes Whisper.

When the world is caving in, She holds the tumbling roof.
Younger than I in years and yet Her wisdom has grown

Like moss on stones over countless lifetimes. Marching to the
tune of no drum,

She engraves Her own path
upon the Earth's skin. And when they
arrive

Wielding sharpened knives and burning torches Crafted from
embers of a dying sunset,

She faces them with a smile. Leaving spite at Her feet, She
steps into battle.

With each stride, Her eyes whisper, "I dare you."

T.J. Jensen -1/24/2018

43.7062996, -114.8975723

Airbrushed sky drapes itself over a pine green canvas.
dripping down the backside of mountains,

it dresses the rocks embedded it's
skin,

and showers the landscape
with color sweeter than wine, poured
from God's own cup.

It is at this special place where bread is broken, and the sins
of the past float with the salmon down the Snake River.

The night sky has seen the love overflowing from the souls
of the outcasts who call this valley home,

And the soles of their shoes imprint
themselves into the dirt, declaring the
soil they stand upon the land of the free
and the home of the yet to be saved.

The blades of grass are watered by
the tears of the lost ones who find
love in the glow of the fire we gather around,
holding one another
like we are all we have ever known.
Here, we are found.
Here, we are saved. Here, we are
free.

T.J. Jensen -2/19/2018

Dear Abella,

The Ocean called to us, as we stood overlooking the end of the world from on high. The mermaidens' cries of passion and understanding could just so slightly be heard over the crushing cacophony of water's gasping breath as it rolled and swirled in on itself before assumedly plummeting its last goodbye as it bellows off some unseen edge into further mysteries.

We passed a glass of wine, old grapes learning new tricks after being mixed with the fires of burning thought, from my rose-stained lips and tongue to your own, as our eyes took in the decaying rays of a sun being set to rest, cooled in the angry waters, only to alight someone else's distant shores.

As the freezing orb set into its watery grave, it gave off colors that permeated the sky in ways similar to how the fine bouquet in our glass had reddened our cheeks with mirth and cognisant underweavings of who we are and why we were here.

In that moment, we understood everything. In that moment, we understood nothing. We were a part of the whole and apart from the whole, beating a 4/4 tempo into the very core of zen appreciation...

After the reflection of that giant ball of brilliance had met its creator and finally settled into the giant pond

laid before us, we continued our mentoring program, letting neither the chill of the biting wind nor the dark of the ever growing
shadow of night deter us from what the world wished to teach our hearts.

There is beauty in a Summer's day, bright and vivid, just as there is a magnificence in the starry night. However, there is also a grand truth to the destruction and creation of these. Every sunset has been a celebration of woes. Every sunrise will be a chance to start anew. These are not choices to be taken or ignored. Instead, they happen whether we appreciate their fine layers or not; whether we watch with our full attention or bury our heads into the sand.

Abella, my heart weeps at every loss I have experienced. From minor scratches to unending wounds, I weep for those I have attached to that small, stubborn organ who have ripped themselves away or I have given away as needed. But so is also true, I am elated at the thought of what will come as the rested sun waves good morning as it breaks free of it nightly confines and starts its daily travel anew. It knows its path and the eventuality of such things, and yet it continues. Because that's why it is here. And it is beautiful.

– Brimo
http://dearabella.wordpress.com

Dear Abella,

Tonight, I stood under the stars for the first time in far too long, dreaming of brighter yesterdays and hesitant tomorrows. As they are want to do, the fears crashed into me from all around. I am too broken, too small of skill and determination, too static, too old... Just too damn old to wash my hands and look for a fresh start in anything more than a flight of fancy or vibrant fantasy. Too old to do more than try to make the path I'm on a little brighter, a little easier to tread. Too old to begin what I should be in the process of wrapping up.

Tonight, I stood under the stars, nothing but a speck on a speck in a sky far too vast and full of wonders for me to ever begin to comprehend, worlds on worlds on worlds of things to do, of things unexplored.

Tonight, I stood under the stars, and for what felt like the first time in years...I took a true, honest breath. And I told those fears to go fuck themselves. I will never be perfect. I will never even be close. But, I can always try to find happiness. I can always remember what it is to be me. Here or there, attached or alone, the only person who can cheat me of a chance for a brighter tomorrow is myself. And I want to love myself enough to give me that chance again.

Tonight, I stood under the stars. And I smiled.

— Brimo
http://dearabella.wordpress.com

Inked hearts

She tattooed
Her fire
And magic
On his soul;
Becoming
A beast
Without a single Wilting
rose
To wish her back...

R ROJA
Poems by Roberto Roja
@sketches_of_madness

Messages from Spain

"Is poetry dead?"
Asked the wind...
"No," replied the sea...
"For as long as they see Love
reflected through us, They
will continue to burn And
write on..."

R ROJA
Poems by Roberto Roja
@sketches_of_madness

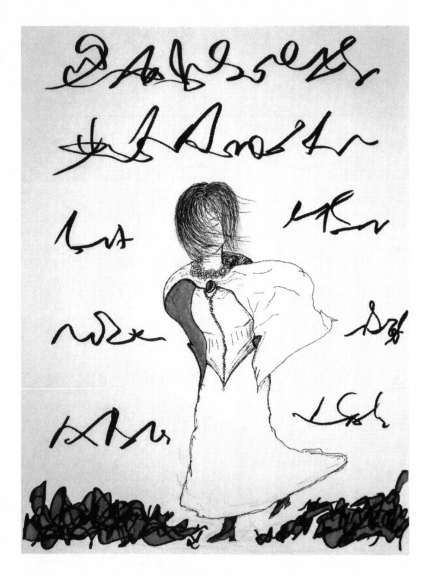

Rebekah Jenks

I could see the disappointment in their eyes-metal hate
regurgitated   from   robotic   mouths,   never
programmed to feel;
 synthetic love imitated with porcelain thoughts, a
precarious reproduction of the real thing;
I could see them-
 fumbling in the dark, searching for something at the
bottom of each other,
leaving behind nothing except
 splinters on thighs from wooden hands that swore he was
a real boy;
  I could see the despair in their eyes-mechanical minds and
                    dormant hearts, never taught to love;
 auto-generated lines spewing from disingenuous lips,
nothing more than
 rote sentiments from autopilot lives, never designed to be
more.

Michael Edwards @___acquiesce

Get me a shovel to bury roses
once they've stopped growing, slashed and severed at the
spinal cord, discarded in dirt graves;
the pursuit of beauty is relentless, and nothing less is
useful;
get me a shovel to build fences-tall fences, stringent grey
palisades, equally as effective
in containment as deflection; get me a shovel
to erect walls,
concrete, cemented hate;
walls that won't fall like nations, more resilient than
marble sculptures of gods that have long since gone; get
me a shovel.

Michael Edwards
@___acquiesce

How do you fill your empty life? if not with tinctures, if not
with trinkets,
if not with worries that wilt your withering will to your wits
end;
how do you feed your empty soul? if not with
discrimination,
if not with masturbation,
if not with validation from bodies, warm bodies, decaying
bodies with coal eyes that smoulder, coal eyes that burn
holes,
ashen holes we poke fingers in; how do you feel whole?
if not with shit, if not with drugs,
legal and illegal drugs, shoved down soft throats, soft
throats that swallow, shoved down slit throats, Slit throats
that bleed and still believe.

Michael Edwards
@___acquiesce

Sestina

I got the news: Will was the first to hang.
His widow told me where and when and how. She knew
not why. I did, but wouldn't say:
A roil of booze and bruise and broken songs
"'Cause I'm the garbage man," Will sang me once. The
trash trail through his heart led to his death.
 For all Tom's life he boldly courted death. Bipolar: sink
and soar, rise up and hang.
He fell in love. We thought him safe but once That fell
apart he had a why and how.
He took the leap and flew into a song.
"Rain falling on my shoe" as Tom would say.
 I can't collect my thoughts enough to say
How dirty, double-dealing demon death
Took Kevin by the hand, to softly sing
Into his ear, I'd like to see you hang.
Now "death don't have no mercy" -- just see how He
took his life, his wife; both lost at once.
 I ran away from home to Margaret once,
When she had moved from green to green. I say I ran
back then but now I run from how
My oldest dear stays ever young in death.
It's still not real. Did such a sister hang
Though "something like a bird within her sang"?
 These lovers four I met after I sang
My own swan song: I dangled, kicking, once.
I was the last to die, the first to hang.
"Into the black" went back to blue, you'd say.

But living in the blue does not cheat death. The
what of life has not taught me the how.
 Time never stopped or slowed. I wonder how Eternity is
bounded by their songs.
My lovers touch me still, through time, past death. I'll
always hold those hearts that pounded once, When limbs
were flesh and mouths had much to say Of sweat, of
breath, updraft where we both hang.
 And though we all did hang you can see how
I dare to say that I alone still sing.
I hanged just once, then lived to drown in death.

Maxfield Sparrow

"Seaside" by Lacy Perrenoud

The Letter V

Ooo whoever's seeing my sweet letter V Make sure
that you treat her nicely
So please don't you be like me
Because then surely you will see
That I hurt my sweet sweet letter V
All that I want is for to be happy
I'm so sorry that I failed to see
All that she really needed me to be
So please don't you be like me
Please don't you hurt my sweet sweet letter V
Because then surely you will see
That you have become just like me
make sure that you treat her nicely
ooo whoever's seeing my sweet letter V

Josh Cobb

MY HEART IS COLD
AND WHEN IT'S NOT
IT JUST HURTS ALONE
I AM HOPE GONE VOID
IS MY LIGHT SO DARK
SOMETIMES
I CAN'T CRY

Poems and Images by J.M Cole @Mydystopia

MYDYSTOPIA®

STILL LOOKING
FOR THAT STAR GOLD
STILL LOOKING INSIDE
LOOKING TO BE THREE
LOOKING TO BE NINE
STILL LOOKING
FOR THAT OCEAN
INSIDE A DREAM
I SEEN
STARS OF GOLD
STARS OF OLD
BLUE AND RED
A TALE UNTOLD
UNFOLDS A ROBE
RED AND GOLD
SNOW COLOURED GLOBE
CAGE IS COLD
INSIDE ALONE
I CLIMB TO BE
I CLIMB TO SEE
A PERFECT CLIMBER
I DREAM
DIAMONDS AND STARS
ARROWS AND DREAD
RED QUESTION
MARKS A SUPANOVA
IMPLODES AFAR.

Poems and Images by J.M Cole @Mydystopia

Poems and Images by J.M Cole @Mydystopia

My phone died on Beale Street, and I didn't care because I could see the music, feel the vibrations, and could hear the things you weren't saying.

Black coffee on a gray morning, the New York City subway is like a hug. A woman smiles at me for no reason. A man falls asleep standing up and wakes up just in time to get off at his stop. There are good people here, packed together, with arms grabbing bars in every direction. Everyone has somewhere to be this morning, but I'm already where I'm supposed to be: Perpetually — in transit, Permanently —transitioning. I never lived in this city, but no one knows but me, because I fit in it, I belong to New York, and it will forever belong to me.

Love is pouring someone a glass of milk while they're eating chocolate chip cookies. It's hugging your best friend when they feel like their life is falling apart. It's cleaning a cut with peroxide and saying, "It will just hurt for a second," then covering it with a bandaid and saying, "All better." Love is unconditional, done on purpose, and never with expectation attached to it. Love is an action, not just a feeling. It's what you do, not just what you say.

I have hope for you. I have hope for me, too. I hope that things will get better before they get worse again. I hope I fall in love, even though I know my heart will break again. I hope I really live before I die. I hope that when I lose hope, someone will give me some of theirs, and I hope they remind me that happy endings are real. But only in stories, because there is a beginning, middle, and end, and our lives are the same, we just have so many stories in a lifetime, they can't all end happily. But God damn it, I hope I enjoy the ones that do!

I like your lipstick. I would call it red. But you would call it so much more than that. There are so many different kind of reds, I'm just ignorant to them. Really, I'm ignorant to you, too. I barely know you. But I want to learn, I want to learn the names of the different reds.

My last night in this bed. Every possession packed in my rental car. The walls are bare. It starts to rain. My car is on a ship. The windows I never cleaned. That one hike I didn't do. The sky diving trip that got cancelled. These thoughts fly through my mind. I'm going home, but this is my home too, this town has been mine for four months, I've been a local in it. I don't want to leave on that plane, but I definitely can't stay here any longer. I try to notice if I've changed, if all this was worth it. I hope it was, I hope I know if it was. I try to sleep, one more night, in this bed.

I'm so sensitive to the world, and I write to try to make sense of it. My stories are always fiction, but my poetry is always real, always honest, and sometimes it's too honest, and I tell people things I shouldn't, and it changes things in my life. People treat me different. Or I confuse them. They don't know if it's real. "What girl is that about?" "Is that really how you feel?" "Is that about me?" It's scary sometimes, but I have to do it, I'd be more scared if I didn't.

-Greg Bee

I will always be okay without you.
But not the same, Never really the same.

E.l.c
Ellie Crowther
@elcdrafts

Darling,
I have never met someone so afraid of what their own
mind can create.
Last night you woke up with body bags under your eyes.

E.l.c
Ellie Crowther
@elcdrafts

I want you to know how much it hurt.
And then I so badly wanted you to know how much it didn't
anymore.

E.l.c
Ellie
Crowther
@elcdrafts

When you finally let yourself fall for someone, I
hope you don't fall too far from yourself.

E.l.c
Ellie Crowther
@elcdrafts

A Last Breath And Twilight

Caught behind the curtains hung by fate
as thick mist across valleys of life
whose paths long unmarked and with traps rife
lay under gone moons risen quite late;

yet misfortune would find, through a glance
into your eyes and their depths of blue,
its last breath and twilight when the true
love that lives inside you took a chance

to project upon dark roads the gleam
of its essence; enraptured as one
rescued lost soul raised above the streams

where death runs, I'd find new springs begun
when a long winter at long last seemed
to take the course of a book that's done...

Daniel Leal @one_song_away

Fall Days

Scattered petals of a red rose raise
high above the ground, upon which tears
washed away the remnants of past fears,
sounds which weave your name into fall days

made to translate into love the wind
whose smooth motion borrowed from your
voice
an ethereal shade to be rejoiced
deep within my heart, for my once bent

spirit saw upon your face the light
long missing from a life I perceived
as water in slow-receding tides

and robbed of the purpose you'd retrieve
when my blind eyes you'd first gently guide
far from fates like those of fallen leaves...

Daniel Leal @one_song_away

December Winds II

When the wind pushed strands of your brown
hair
off your shoulders as the day grew cold,
it still felt like the first time your hold
on my soul tinged the December air

with the soothing textures of your palms,
as your fingertips drew smooth outlines
of dreams which in my sleep left no sign
of smiles then set to become the balm

flowing as the sense, which through your gift
to my shattered heart, brought me much more
than just noble thoughts that caused a shift

in the essence of life and its lore;
much as your love, through my spirit, drifts
as the sun would on deep-ocean floors...

Daniel Leal @one_song_away

A Silhouette at Dusk (The Day After Your
Birthday IV)

If I were to tell heavens from days
whose light descends slowly into dark
only to reveal upon your face
clearly defined flames your inner spark

stretches across the chill of a life
to be found wanting without your heart
as the substance on which mine can thrive
so long as the choice to never part

with the love you need never return,
as my act of defiance of death,
remains all my own flames need to burn,

would a single word require breath
when nothing has been left to discern
between such days, your eyes and their depth?

Daniel Leal @one_song_away

We

We're the passable music that we hear We,
we're the stories that we share We're the
silences that creep
In our closets when we sleep.
We're the smells of our cologne
The hypocrites that we've grown
Into. We're the directionless compasses
Nobody told us but we're on our own. We're
moths of the momentary Dancing 'bout fires
of responsibilities Passengers of fate
In a sea of perishable identities.

@Illuminatus

Dear Future Self

Dear ignorant future self,
Stop telling me, "It's fine."
I'm fed up. It is here that I
Draw the line.
Refrain from all suggestions
You might have up your sleeve
Stop acting like an upgrade of me
A mature guardian, I ought to believe.
I'm figuring it out for you
Just let me, for once, if you could
Maybe I'm clueless and depressed but
It's for your, nay, OUR greater good.
Dear ignorant future self "It's all going to work out." I
know that to be true Hold just one thought
In that little chill brain of yours
That I made you,
YOU.

@Illuminatus

I Forgive You

"I forgive you"

I eat these words every day
And they taste a lot like your kisses Bitter
Sweet
"I forgive you" My soul

Refuses to swallow the lies I tell myself But my lips Savor
every word My tongue
Taste every syllable
And they taste a lot like your kisses Bitter
Sweet
"I forgive you"

Maybe if I keep eating these words Then one day

my Soul will learn How to swallow these words

How to believe these words How to swallow these words
Like she once believed the "I love yous" That escaped
your lips
Bitter
Sweet
But she always swallowed
Because they gave her the energy to keep loving you
But now "I forgive you"

Only gets stuck between my teeth

Dries up my throat when I try to swallow Because my
soul knows that these
Are just lies I tell myself

"I forgive you"

Maybe if I keep saying these words Then one day I'll learn
how to believe these words "I forgive you" "I forgive you"
"I forgive you" "I forgive you" But these words
Keep getting stuck between my teeth Dries up my throat
when I try to swallow Because I'm still angry Still hurting
Still haven't forgiven myself
How could you do this to me

I did everything I could to keep you

Held on tightly even when everything in me Wanted to let
you go
And that's why I haven't forgiven myself Yet Because
deep inside
I knew I should have never held on so tightly Deep inside
I knew that you did not deserve the energy I gave you
And that's why my soul refuses to swallow "I forgive you"
Even though I need to swallow these words For the
energy to love myself
But my soul would rather starve than get fed Because
once upon a time she
Fed off
The "I love yous" that escaped your lips Bitter Sweet
But she always swallowed
Because they gave her the energy To
keep loving you

But now
She won't even swallow "I forgive you" Because she still
craves for your "I love yous" So she can
Spit them in your face
Make you feel how you made her feel Broken Small
Never enough
But "I forgive you"

Because not forgiving you hurts me more

But my soul

My soul would rather starve
Because how can she swallow "I forgive you" When she still
hasn't forgiven herself
For letting you see so much of her Even though your kisses
were Bitter
Sweet
Just like your "I love yous"

By Zerbine Atosha Rypa

Desperate souls

Call acts of violence Justified reaction,
Aim with their remaining eye To blind a rival faction.

"The ends justifies the means" They say to you and I.

I can excuse expatriates To dream- but not to lie.

The ends do not affect the means. The means becomes
the end,

At least, an end as real to some As that one you defend.

To break the turning wheel of pain, First heal the wound
you know.
Let love attest. Forgive the rest. Allow new skin to grow.

-Andrew Calvin Timmons
(@andcaltim)

You've made mistakes And that's okay

You don't need permission To be human

You're afraid of something And that's okay Courage

requires fear

You can want to be better And still be enough

To love yourself today

Allow yourself

To live and learn
Love as you would be loved There is nothing wrong With
loving who you are Hear me

You are enough You always were

-Andrew Calvin Timmons
(@andcaltim)

Men are more comfortable With the idea of pain. Women, on the other hand,

Have a much higher tolerance for it. But why should this be surprising? Women have always been

More tolerant of many things. First they had to be, Then they chose to be,

But that was misinterpreted It seems

Long suffering is a feminine tongue Women must translate For certain men to understand That their tolerance was kindness And kindness isn't weakness. Perhaps they must explain it

In a way men find more "Comfortable"

-Andrew Calvin Timmons
(@andcaltim)

Sierra Foerster

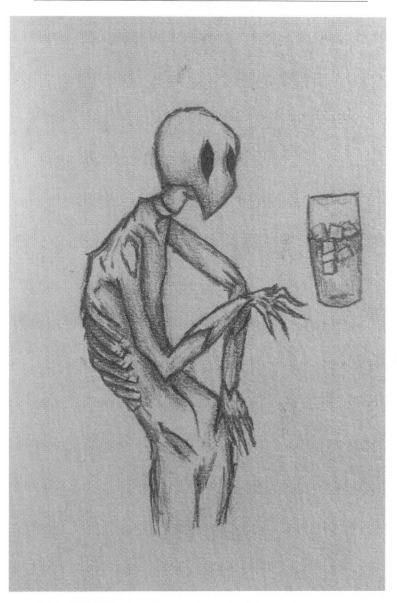

Sierra Foerster

Sierra Foerster

A Little Dream
By Jareth Sampson

Dedra loved this part of town. It was so quiet at night. All of the trees along the sidewalk glowed with Christmas lights. The snow crunched under her soft, wool lined, boots. Though there was still a month left until Christmas, she half expected to see Saint Nick flying about overhead, reindeer dragging his tremendous behind through the heavens. It was the perfect night for a walk.

Out of nowhere came the clicking, chomp of boots on concrete through snow. She looked over her shoulder to see a man walking behind her. He wore a long black coat, thick soled boots, worn jeans, and a black t-shirt. His head was down, the brim of his gray, felt, hat shielding his features. His left hand was in his pocket, and his right held a brown papered cigarette, its end glowing brightly in the shadow of his sleeve. He raised the cigarette to his face, revealing his lips and a well groomed beard, and took a long drag, smoke billowing out a moment later. Dedra just kept walking, turning the corner at her next opportunity, going deeper into the Old Town district. The man turned as well. She looked back at him as she approached the end of the next block, turning again and going back the way she'd come. Again, the man turned. He flicked the glowing butt of his cigarette out into the street as Dedra turned yet again, this time hoping to see another person.

More empty sidewalk lay before her. As she reached an intersection she rushed across the street, disobeying the DONT WALK command blinking above the snow covered asphalt. The man kept pace, despite the fact that he seemed to be moving at the same speed as before. "He's just some asshole." She mumbled and kept walking. Finally, the sound of his boots hitting the cold pavement in time with the thud of her heart became too much to handle. She stopped and spun. The man stopped as well, his head still down, but she could see a smile as he lit a second cigarette with a copper Zippo. "Who the hell are you?" she asked. The man put the Zippo away and took a long drag on the cigarette, holding the smoke. "Did someone put you up to this?" She shouted. The man responded with a chuckle that billowed smoke. "Say something you son-of-a-bitch, or I'm calling the police!" and the man did speak, in a sense.

"Stars shining bright above you." he began to sing. Dedra recognized the tune, but couldn't place it. "Sweet breezes seem to whisper, I love you." His voice was deep, powerful, and gentle, but incredibly unsettling in the still street. "Birds singing in the sycamore tree," he crooned, taking a step toward her as he puffed on the cigarette again, flicking it into the street. "Dream a little dream of me." She knew the song! Her mother used to sing it to her when she was a little girl.

"Who the hell are you?" she asked taking a step back.

"Say nighty-night and kiss me. Just hold me tight and tell me you'll miss me." He sang, walking toward her now, his hands flexing at his sides. He reached into the coat and pulled a long dagger out of a shoulder sheath. Dedra couldn't run. She was frozen in place. Fear had paralyzed her. "While I'm alone, blue as can be," he got closer and closer. Run! Her instincts screamed. Get out of here! Run for it Dedra! But she was far too afraid to listen. The man was almost upon her when Dedra felt an arm wrap around her waist and pull her back. She looked up and saw a tall man, his short, black hair hung over his forehead. His skin was pale and was a good contrast to the neat little goatee decorating his chin. He wore brown work boots and a leather jacket. At the end of the sleeve that wasn't wrapped around her was a gun, held in a substantial mitt, aimed at the man in the felt hat.

"Piss off, or I shoot!" Yelled the man in leather, and the man in the hat stopped, began to back-step, and then dashed around the corner. "You okay miss?" the man in leather lowered her gently into the snow. Her jeans were getting soaked, but she didn't care. She was alive!

"I am now. Thank you. I was so scared!" She leaned into his warm chest and began to sob. He patted her head and shushed her soothingly. "The worst part was he just kept singing this song that my mother used to sing. I haven't heard it since... and that bastard-" the man in leather put his head down, mumbled something, and his shoulders started to shake as if he were crying. A sick feeling came over Dedra, bile rising in her throat. "What did you say?"

He looked up, a thick smile on his face, teeth showing. "Dream a little dream of me." He whispered the song, each note distinct, perfectly on pitch despite his low voice.

"How did you-" He began to whistle the song to her and she jumped up, backing away. "Stop that right now!" and he did, but she heard the whistling continue behind her. She turned and the man with the felt hat brought his knife across hard, cutting a clean line through her throat. She turned, clutching at her broken trachea, and stumbled straight into the muzzle of the other man's gun. The leather of his jacket creaked as he pressed it between her eyes. Her heart beat blood out of her throat and onto his clean, white shirt. She let out a wet gurgle that was meant to be a scream.

"Dream a little dream of me." the men sang together in perfect harmony as the shot fired and everything went dark for Dedra.

Her heart was pounding when she woke. Every inch of her was drenched in sweat; her thin nightclothes clinging to her skin. Her breaths came in gasps. It had been a dream. A horrible dream. She sighed, climbed out of her bed, and left the room, intent on water. She walked into the kitchen and ran a glass from the tap, gulping it down in one swallow. She pressed her hands to the front of the counter and looked out into the night from her third story apartment. Under a streetlamp, staring up at her from ground level stood a man with black hair. A little goatee decorated his chin. He wore brown work boots and a leather jacket. He seemed to be staring right at her, a cigarette in his smile, and hands in pockets.

"Jesus!" she cursed and stepped away from the window, gasping for breath, when she hit something solid and felt the cold blade of a knife against her throat. A hand pressed her head back against a shoulder and she felt the scratch of a beard on her cheek. Her eyes flicked over, seeing only the brim of a gray, fedora-like, felt hat and a pair of smiling, cracked lips. She could smell the smoke on them. The lips backed up, pressing to her ear as the knife bit into her skin. "Dream a little dream of me."

Dedications:

To my Mother, for giving me strength, and everything else.

To my Grandparents, for your constant love and encouragement.

To my little sisters, for inspiring me and giving me a reason to keep going.

To J.S. for bringing me back to life and for loving me even on my worst days.

To my publisher, for her brilliant work and above all her patience.

To everyone I have loved, and everyone that has hurt me...you gave me something to write about.

To you, dear reader...because without someone to read it, what good would poetry be?

Thank you. This is for you.

-Kabrie